THANKSGIVING
PIANO SONGS

TOP 20
POPULAR CLASSIC MUSIC

FOR BEGINNERS

THANKSGIVING

Piano Songs

Top 20 Popular Classic Music

for Beginners

Arranged by *Alicja Urbanowicz*

CONTENTS:

Amazing Grace

John Newton

Moderato

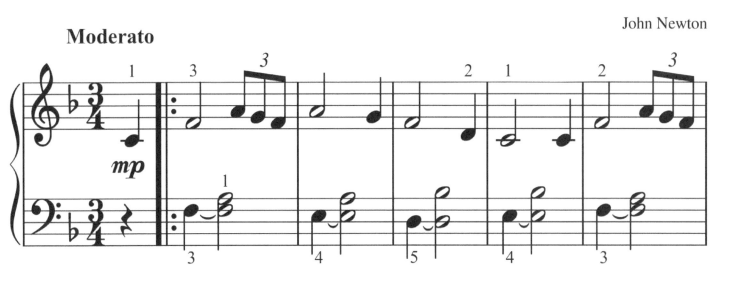

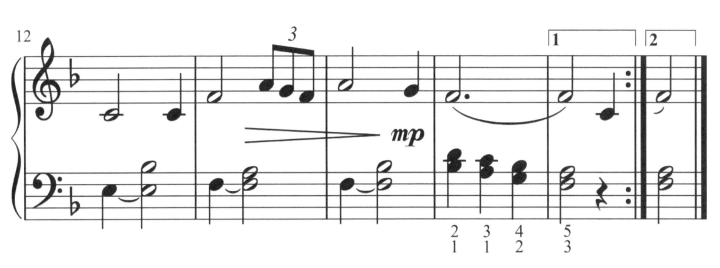

Turkish March

W. A. Mozart

Allegretto

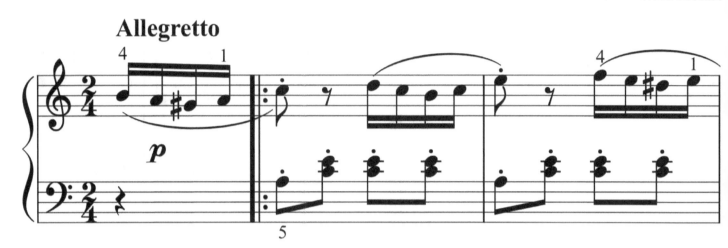

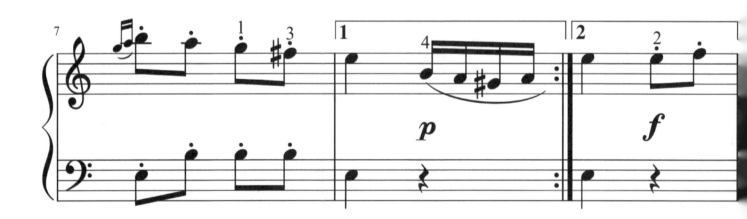

Fur Elise

Ludwig van Beethoven

Ped. simile

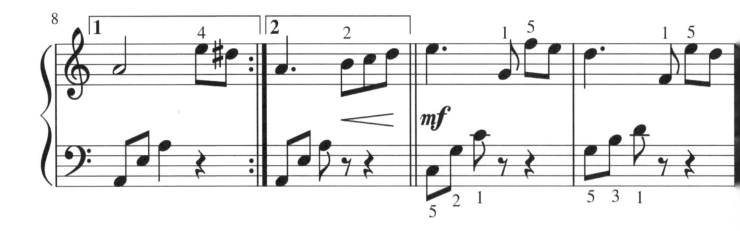

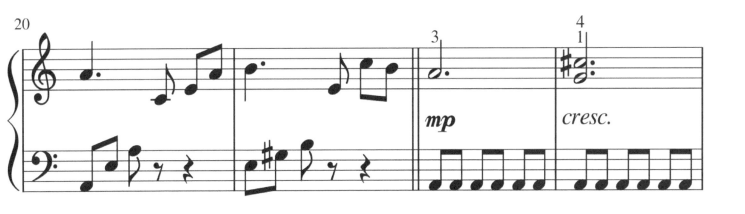

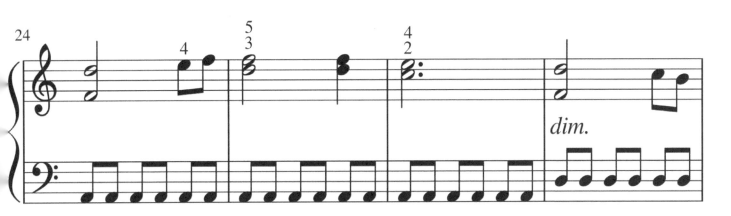

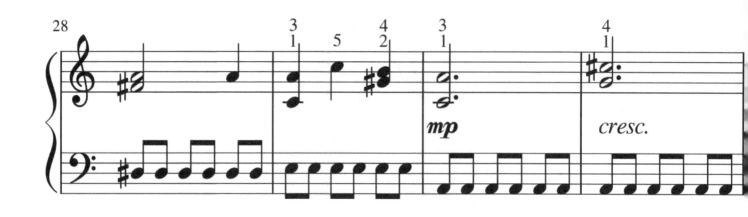

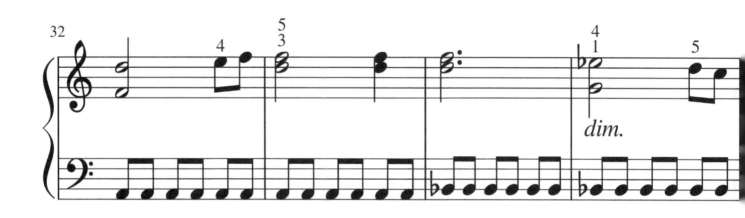

Jesu, Joy of Man's Desiring

from Cantata BWV147

J. S. Bach

Moderato

1

Pathetique Sonata

2nd Movement

Ludwig van Beethoven

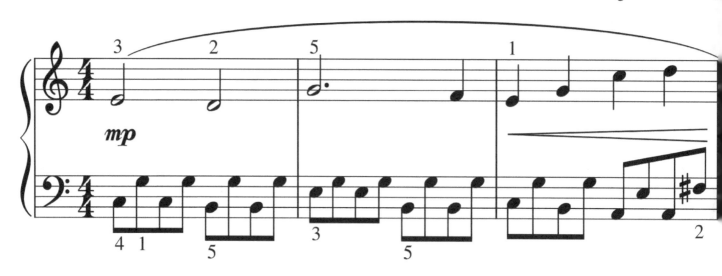

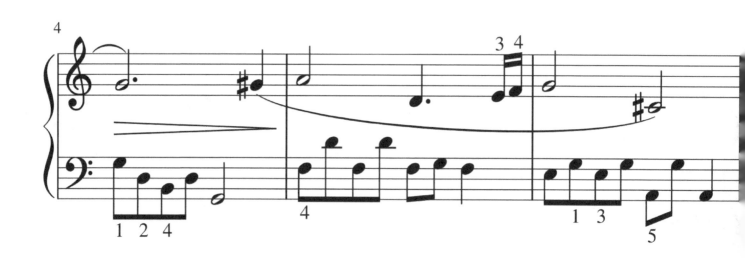

16

Ave Maria

Franz Schubert

Andante

18

Canon in D

Johann Pachelbel

23

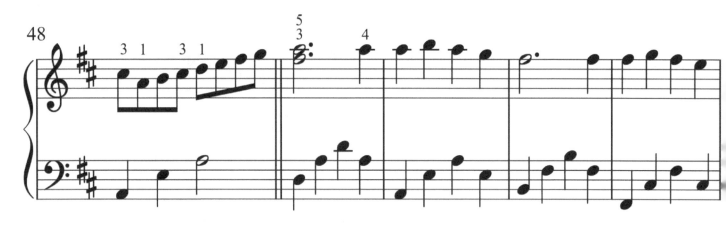

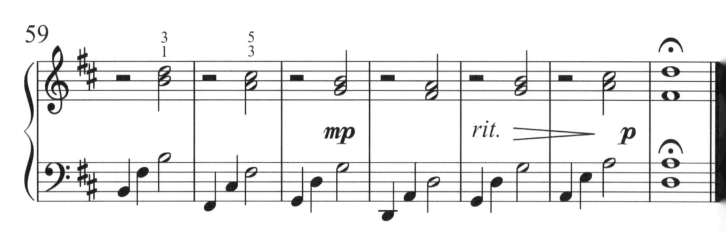

Clair de Lune

Andante

Claude Debussy

Holy, Holy, Holy

John B. Dykes

Joy to the World

George F. Handel

Morning Mood
from Peer Gynt Suite No. 1

Edvard Grieg

Swan Lake

Peter Ilyich Tchaikovsky

Moderato

Greensleeves

English Folksong

Gymnopedie No. 1

from Trois Gymnopedies

Erik Satie

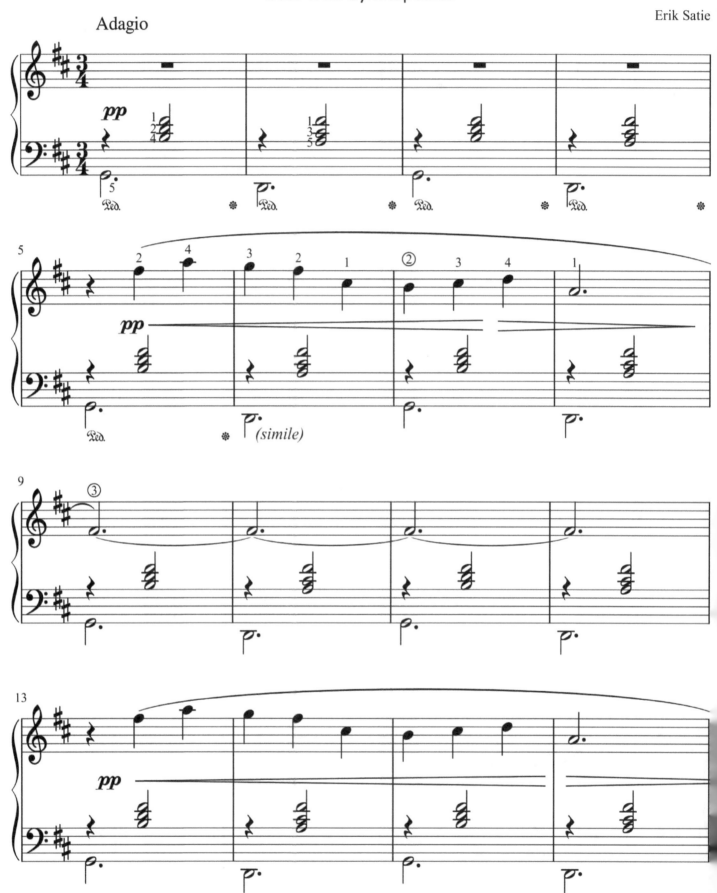

Moonlight Sonata

(Sonata quasi una Fantasia) Op. 27 No. 2.

Ludwig van Beethoven

Liebestraum
from Nocturne No. 3

Franz Liszt

Ode To Joy

Ludwig van Beethoven

Solveig's Song

from Peer Gynt Suite No. 2

Edvard Grieg

Andante

Prelude in C Major

BWV 846

J. S. Bach

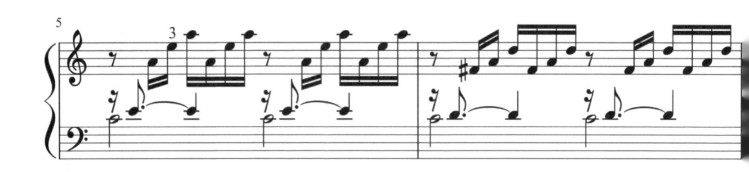

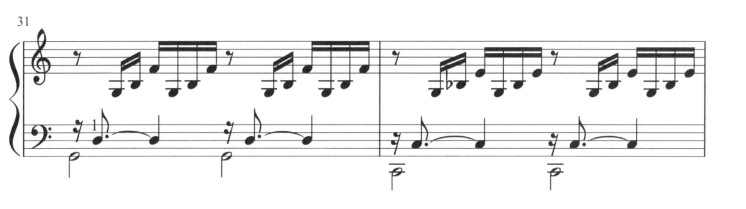

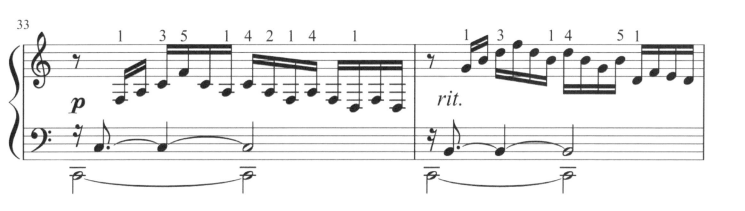

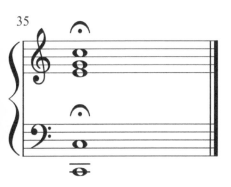

When The Saints Go Marching In

Gospel Piano Solo

Traditional

I want you to enjoy the moment while you play during every special event.

PLEASE REVIEW
THIS BOOK

Alicja Urbanowicz

See other of my easy arrangements for piano.

Made in United States
Troutdale, OR
11/23/2024